City on Ice

Matt Sims

High Noon Books
Novato, California

Editor: Deb Akers
Cover Design: Bonni Gatter
Cover Photographs: courtesy of National Science Foundation/United States Antarctic Program and NASA
Interior Photographs: courtesy of NASA/Jim Ross (3), NASA (9), the National Science Foundation/United States Antarctic Program (14, 19, 23)

High Noon Books
a division of Academic Therapy Publications
20 Commercial Blvd.
Novato, CA 94949-6191

International Standard Book Number: 978-1-57128-478-5

18 17 16 15 14 13 12 11 10 09
10 09 08 07 06 05 04 03 02 01

You'll enjoy all the High Noon Books. Write for a free full list of titles or visit our website at www.HighNoonBooks.com.

Contents

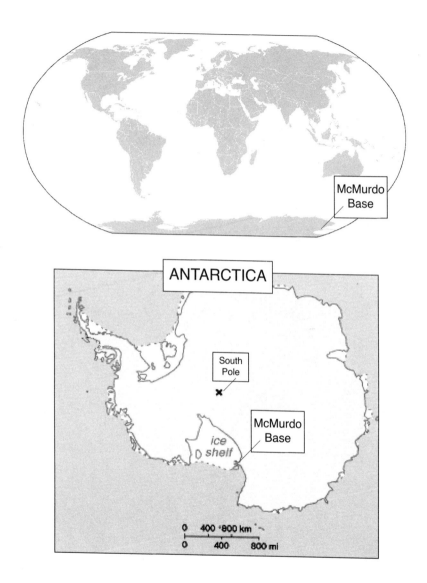

The Ice

The South Pole is the coldest place on Earth. No trees grow there. Big sheets of ice stretch over the land. That ice can be three miles thick.

The South Pole can get as cold as $-100°$. The

winds blow at 200 miles an hour. People call this place the Ice.

Many sea birds and seals live around the South Pole. They fish for food. The seals have fat and fur that keeps them warm.

People have a much harder time on the Ice. We do not have enough

*The South Pole is the coldest place on Earth.
No trees grow there.*

hair to keep us warm.
We often do not have
much fat on us. It is easy
for people to freeze when
it is cold.

Why would anyone
want to live on the South
Pole? The truth is, the
Ice is not a good place for
most people. It takes
someone who can brave
the cold and wind of the

South Pole.

There are people who dream of living on the South Pole. They train to be strong enough to live in the cold. There is a place for these people on the South Pole. It is a small city on the Ice.

Mac

Many people want to learn about the South Pole. Only some of them get to go there. McMurdo Base was built as a place for people to study the South Pole. People call the place "Mac" for short.

The Mac base is the largest town on the South Pole. It is built on a large, bare rock. At first it was just a few huts and buildings. Now the Mac base has 100 buildings.

There are only two ways to get to the Mac. There is an air strip close by. But planes can only land when the skies are clear. That is only a few months of the year!

The Mac base is right by the sea. Each year, a boat called the Green Wave comes to the base. The Green Wave has food and other things for people at the base. But first, it has to break through the sea ice.

The Mac base is the largest town on the South Pole. It is built on a large, bare rock.

A Coast Guard ship called the Polar Star carves a path through the ice. Then the Green Wave lands at the base. Sometimes the ship cannot make it through. Then the people at Mac have to thaw hot dogs from the freezer to eat!

A Place to Learn

The first man to live on
the Ice was named Scott.
He and his crew came to
the South Pole on a ship.
They spent six cold
months on the South
Pole.

Scott built a hut to

live in. But the hut was not built well. It was drafty and very, very cold. The crew gave up and went back to their ship.

But the ship would not move. It was stuck in the ice! Scott and his crew had to camp out for many cold months on their boat.

The crew went out on short trips to look at the land of the South Pole. What they saw made them want to know more about this strange place.

Today, as many as 1,000 people live at the Mac base. They are there to learn about the South Pole. They hike out and watch sea birds and

Scott built a hut to live in.

seals. They cross ice fields and climb steep cliffs. They pick up chunks of rock or ice. They take the pieces back to the base.

The base has labs where people look at what they have found. This is a great way to learn more about life on the South Pole.

A Day in the Life

In some ways, the Mac base is like any other city. There are lights. There are pipes for water. There are phones. Since the base is built on rock, all of these lines and pipes run above ground.

The base has a place to check out books. There is also a fire house with trucks. There is a place to go if you get sick. You can even go bowling if you want!

But the Mac base is not like any other city. People have to spend a lot of time inside. Even in summer the South Pole is only 30°. There are 18 hours of sun light. But in winter, you hardly see the sun at all.

There are few plants and no trees on the South Pole. The people miss seeing green plants. So they built a green house on the Mac base.

Now people can grow

The people miss seeing green plants. So they built a green house on the Mac base.

things to eat. But they mostly like to come and sit in the green house. They like to look at the bright green leaves of the plants. They like feeling the moist, soft air. It helps them feel like they are still on Earth, and not the moon!

Work and Play Hard

Life on the Mac base can be hard. People work ten hours a day. They work six days a week.

People do get outside the base and go on hikes. But the land around the Mac base is full of ice holes. A hiker could fall in a hole. Hikers have to tell the others when they will be back. If they are not back in time, a crew goes out to search.

Some say the hardest part of living at the Mac base is having fun! When it is time to play, there is not much to do. So the Mac staff makes their

If they are not back in time, a crew goes out to search.

own fun.

One fun thing is the Ice Run. People jump in the icy sea in their swim suits!

Is it ever cold! Then the group gets in a big hot tub. The Mac staff plans these kinds of fun things each year. It helps them get through the long, cold months.

Hopes and Dreams

The Mac staff tries to make sure that they do not hurt the land around the South Pole.

People try to reuse things. They leave no trash on the base.

Someone had the

thought of getting dirt bikes to ride around the base. Bikes do not mess up the air like trucks. Now many people ride bikes at the Mac base.

Life at the South Pole can teach us about how the Earth works.

In past years, the Mac staff has watched the ice cap on the South Pole.

That ice is melting. This is very bad news for people. If the ice keeps melting, the sea will get higher. Life on Earth will not be the same.

The staff at Mac base hopes to teach people to take care of the Earth. Their dream is a clean, safe Earth for all living things.

High Frequency Words

an	is	there
and	it	they
around	just	this
as	live	three
be	many	two
call	no	us
can	of	want
do	on	was
for	over	we
get	that	who
good	the	why
have	them	would